LETTERS OF LIFE

Whispers, Secrets, & Lies

LETTERS OF LIFE

OF LIFE

Whispers, Secrets, & Lies

VERNON A. NEALY

ARPress
ILLUMINATING IDEAS.
EMPOWERING VOICES

ARPress
45 Dan Road Suite 5
Canton, MA 02021

Hotline: 1(888) 821-0229
Fax: 1(508) 545-7580

Ordering Information:
Quantity sales. Special discounts are available on quantity purchases by corporations, associations, and others. For details, contact the publisher at the address above.

Printed in the United States of America.

ISBN-13:   Softcover   979-8-89356-444-0
            eBook   979-8-89356-443-3

Library of Congress Control Number: 2024904720

CONTENTS

DEDICATION

This book is dedicated to my grandmother, Mrs. Lucinda Bracey,
for her unconditional love and commitment
and wisdom and her belief in me.

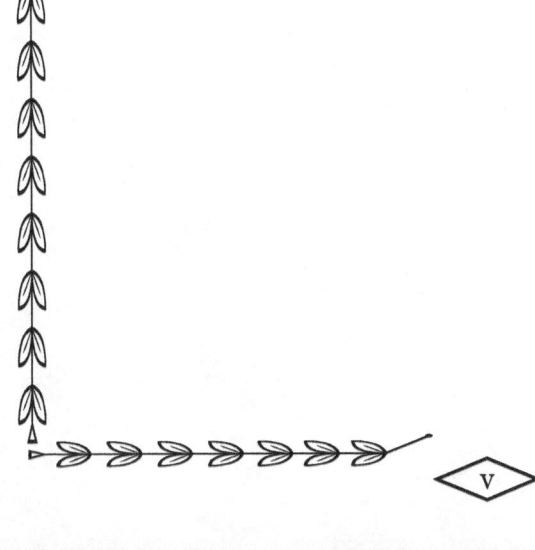

My poetry openly provides insight into understanding life's entanglements. The mind and soul are integral parts which lend themselves to the fundamental moral values expressed by the heart. Beneath the surface of these memoirs lies a parable of verity, which is fitting. Truth harbors no excuse, nor does it answer to anyone.

It is of itself by far the most emancipated attribute of all. For in truth, there is love. In love, there is understanding. In understanding, there is forgiveness. Whispers will cease, Secrets will be revealed, and Lies will manifest themselves, but the truth shall remain evident.

PROVERBS

Chapter One, verse five
A wise man will hear, and increase learning; and a man of
understanding shall attain unto wise counsel.

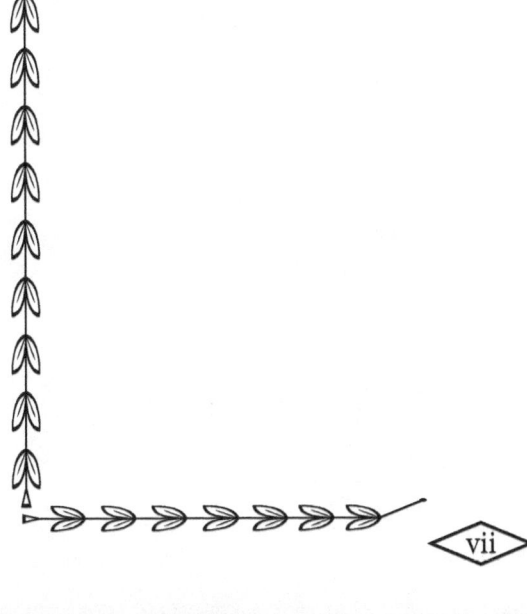

WHISPERS

(hwis´per, wis´-) v. 1. To speak or utter softly, without full voice.

Whispers can be truths or falsehoods... which are uttered from one person to another, or groups of people. They are generally revealed in a low to soft voice, prohibiting anyone within the surrounding area from hearing or eavesdropping. The poems in this section reflect those things that people will discourse under their breath.

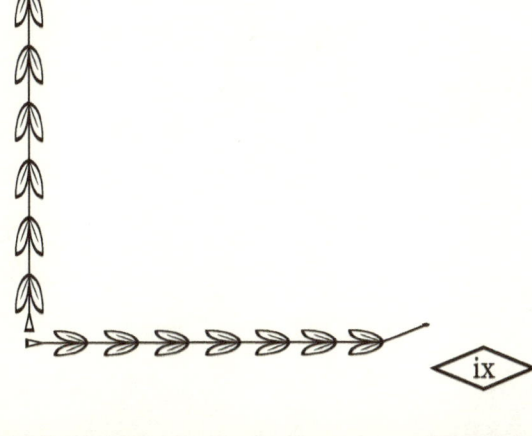

A FATHER'S LOVE

A father's love
Is God's special gift,
Favor handed down
To the children he's with.
He lovingly shelters and protects
As posterity begins to grow,
Providing the warmth accompanied with love
And to every heart the glow.
Understanding along with patience
With a firm teaching hand,
Discipline and obedience
Are part of the master plan.
A father's love
Is an ear that listens,
A shoulder to cry on
And a smile that glistens.
He will comfort his children
In their time of need,
Giving advice
Or planting a seed.
A father's love Is always there,
Despite the odds
He has enough to share
A gift that is special
Blessed from heaven above
Providing what we need
In a father's Love.

Vernon A. Nealy

A MOTHER'S LOVE

Of all the precious gifts
That a family can receive,
Accepting a Mother's Love
Is a love you can believe.
It cradles you from birth
More precious than a pearl,
With nurturing, patience, and understanding
Protecting from the world.
In her eyes lies the care she gives
That's always shining through,
In her smile the pride she has
That says, I'm proud of you.
Her arms do hold with passion
Embracing your gentle frame,
No matter how deep or intense the hurt
She can always ease the pain.
I love you, Mom, with all my heart
Whether you're with us or above,
I'll carry with me your remembrance
And this prayer of a Mother's Love.

A POEM FOR HER

To set aside the rising sun
Accepting the challenge no man has won,
To move a mountain all for your pleasure
Parting a sea that reveals hidden treasure.

All of these miracles I performed for you
Except to caress your heart so blue,
Perhaps it pains for another so dear
Or the need for love and not having it near.

Or is it a secret I'm not to learn
Feeling your pain I'm genuinely concerned,
The mountain, the treasure, all seems so small
To accomplish these wonders means nothing at all.

I would let it all go because that's my style
To witness the warmth of your captivating smile,
Except for these feelings I hold so true
Let these words express how I feel for you.

Vernon A. Nealy

A WOMAN'S HEART

A woman's heart
Will somehow endure,
To live, to love,
And progressively mature
Into a giving, caring,
And wonderful thing,
Expressed by emotions
And the love that it brings.
For the man who honors
Its position,
Total surrender
Without condition.
Understanding her feelings
That will nurture his own,
Protecting and loving
In building her home.

BODY HEAT

Like the embers of a fire
That generate warmth and burn,
Body heat is different
It begins with an erotic yearn.
A soft and gentle whisper
Close enough to feel,
Soft and tender bellowing
Gives an arousing appeal.
Desires begin to inflame
You can see it in the eyes,
Surrendering over the passion
The heat begins to rise.
Moisture blankets the skin
As it becomes increasingly wet,
Temperatures rising higher
Turning it all to sweat.
In the heat of steaming passion
Two hearts, one roaring flame,
Consuming all intentions
Calling it by name.
Sensual, erotic, and carnal,
A level of progressive repeat,
It all falls under the guise
Known as body heat.

CELEBRATION OF LIFE

The revelry has already begun
Don't keep humanity waiting,
A festive time for all who join
And it's yours just for the taking.
The mind is opened and the heart is free
There are no status clicks,
A love for life and the joy it brings
You'll find it all in the mix.
Of course you'll meet the poopers
Manipulative and devilishly coy,
It's their job to win your trust
And steal your hope and joy.
But life overrides such boundaries
Come on in and experience the fun,
The revelry expects your presence
The celebration has already begun.

COLD AROUND THE HEART

To generate warmth
That fills a need,
There is knowledge and wisdom
On which to feed.
Coming from one
Who serves the collective,
My rendering now
Has become ineffective.
In the field of emotions
I search to find
People who are receptive
Loving and kind.
Instead I'm surrounded
In whole or in part,
By those spawning cold
Around the heart.

CONNECTIONS

Examine the scope of humanity
From the beginning of life until death,
You'll find a link that far exceeds
Its height, width, and breadth.

Incomprehensible for some it seems
Yet, most will understand,
An adjunct nexus that bonds the soul
Of every woman, child, and man.

You refer to them as connections
Which we experience from day to day,
Between family and friends or coworkers alike
Understanding what they say.

It may be the language of body or sign,
Even speaking the verbal word,
The connections we make and the steps we take
Making sure that we are heard.

DESIRE

Softly and gently came the warm summer breeze
I watched from my terrace as it swayed the trees,
Memories still vivid from hours before
She stood so inviting on my bedroom floor.
Her hair fiery red like the devil's eyes
Draped in a sheer lace robe,
That exposed her thighs.
I was enchanted by the mystery that carried her song
A melody of broken hearts who have died and gone on.
To a place from which there is no return
Lonely hearts craving love,
Instead they burn.
Oh how cruel can this lovely creature be
Yet, it's her beauty that bewitches me.
All that I have seen and my soul does feel,
Validates this mystery as being real.
But there is something here I can't explain
Urging me on, calling my name.
She extends her arms, wanting to caress
As the passion swells within my chest,
As I fade from reality and into this dream
My consciousness is rocked at the very seam.
Where did she come from, what does it all mean?
Then I remembered the mystery that invoked this dream.
You'll not have me, I'll not play your game,
It's clear to me now I know your name.
You flaunt your wares, twists men's fate
Reaching to embrace their soul you take.
Born out of a need of passion and fire,
You're the devilish vixen known as desire.

DISCLOSURE

Your life will literally be opened
For everyone to see
Just what secret you harbor inside
Once you've spoken to me.
A shunning by your peers
For a character that's too loose,
All will begin to take effect
When you reveal the truth.
Be careful what and how you say it
And whomever you may involve,
A confession that has no integrity
Is not that easily resolved.
Choose your battles fittingly
Make sure you don't get burned,
A disclosure of a personal nature
The tables can easily turn.
Wanting to be free
So this burden you expose,
Choose a person you really trust
Before you begin to disclose.

DREAMS

Wonders of the imagination
Inspired by hope and love,
A vision brought into reality
With the perspiration they're of…
Thought, toil, and patience to spare
Adding consistency too,
A belief in oneself
Who never gives up
Will make your dreams come true.
Keeping in mind the focus
To attain it you must have the means,
Use them wisely and use them well
Or they are no better than dreams.

DREAMS ARE

Aspirations and desires of the heart
In which you must firmly believe,
Ideas must work through the mind and arms
If they are ever to be achieved.

With vision you can see it
When others don't,
On faith you can do it
When others won't
Dreams are.

ENCHANTMENT

With all the appeal of a fairy tale
The first kiss is where it begins,
The closeness, the warmth, the feeling you get
Who would guess we started as friends.

Becoming very compassionate
To what we've felt in part,
Emotions don't lie
They speak from the heart.

We can hide them, bide them
Or even disguise them,
But sooner or later
We cannot deny them,

It's the allure of an apple
Or quest for the ring,
The amazement it inspires
Enchantment will surely bring.

So, indulge yourself
Let those feelings descend,
Your fairy tale starts
When the first kiss begins.

FOR ALL SEASONS

To practice patience and respect
Some people need a reason,
Extending warmth from day to day
For some it just is not pleasin'

They are taken off a shelf
And put on display,
Embracing virtuous traits
On any given day.

It seems to have significance
They think it looks so good,
Actually, it is hypocritical
And often misunderstood.

So, for you as a person
To be kind you need a reason?
Acquire the patience and learn respect
Then use them for all reasons.

FRIENDSHIP

Soft and delicate
As the petal of a rose,
The bonding of spirits
Begins to grow.

Challenging your strengths
And constitution,
Finding the chemistry
With the right solution.

Discovering devotion
Acknowledging limitations,
Setting the stage
For a strong foundation.

Experiencing the warmth
And not letting it slip,
Initiating the journey
Consummating friendship.

GRIEF

As sadness befalls
The heart is weighted down.
A burden that the shoulders
Cannot bear because they're bound.
The mind becomes clouded
The soul begins to wail,
Life now is obscured
By a shroud or a veil.
In the waters you drift
Saddled with the fears,
Floating helplessly downstream
Into a river of tears.
The heart now begins to melt
The next step is hard to take,
Finding yourself sinking
To a much lower state.
All this and more
As you journey beyond belief,
You have entered the realm
And a state of grief.

I CRY

As I exile myself
And begin to sigh,
In the quiet of my loneliness
I start to cry.
Pondering the mistakes
Of decisions and fears,
No one can see
The streams of tears.
Loves challenged, and loves lost,
I entered the game,
Longing for a heart
Instead I feel pain.
Why must I hurt?
When it's love that I seek,
It escapes my grasp
Uncontrollable I weep.
But here in my sorrow
I begin to cope,
Clinging to desire
Believing in hope.
For tomorrow I live again
And again I shall try,
If unsuccessful then
Again I will cry.

I'M SORRY

These words are often difficult
To think of much less say,
Having to convey my sentiments
In an honest and remorseful way.
It is very hard to explain
When I know what I did was wrong,
Concealing this dishonesty
I've had for so long.
Knowing eventually you would find out
About this hideous and deceitful play,
Taking advantage of you
In an unjust and spiteful way.
But herein lies the truth
All the blame I do accept,
Being honest as well as sincere
As I stand before you correct.
I make no frivolous excuses
For my behavior I am contrite,
I am sorry and I do apologize
As I stand here in your sight.

IF I COULD WEEP

If I could weep, it would be
For the homeless lady,
Or the girl who just
Lost her baby.

All the fathers who
Have lost their sons,
A noble contribution
Their deeds are done.

Or a sister whose brother
Has died on the streets,
A mother whose daughter
Grants midnight treats.

The severity of each case
Engulfs the heart so quick,
If you fail to understand
Add yours to the mix.

If I could weep
What a river I would cry,
Overflowing the eyelids
Beginning with a sigh.

Feeling the pain
And claiming to own it,
The hurt filled with tears
For each passing moment.
Yes, if I could weep.

IT'S TIME TO GET REAL

To sing the songs
That others have sung,
Claiming the victories
Others have won.
Acknowledging before men
In your presence they must kneel,
You'll know when I say
It's time to get real.
This faÃ§ade you wear
Like a shimmering crown
Will lose its luster
When others have found
You lie, you cheat
Trying to conceal
And have them believe
That's part of the deal.
But this heart-to-heart
Is between you and I
That exterior you exhibit
I just don't buy.
My advice to you, get rid of that zeal,
Learn what truth is
Then, it's time to get real

JUSTICE

On the verge of conventional truth
Man harbors on the bane,
For it's his peers he tends to please
Who give reverence to his name.

But what a perpetual web we spin
With hypocrisy as our mask,
To extend our cup with society filling it up
Equity is what we ask.

LEADERSHIP

When you fill your vision with aspirations
Your soul will never tire,
Only a few accepting the challenge
Of greater heights to aspire.
It is those to whom we look upon
Who guide our way with courage,
With faith and trust, following their lead
It will keep you from becoming discouraged.
Either male or female can fit the bill
As long as the job gets done,
Giving credit where credit is due
It's their leadership that has won
Maybe you have just what it takes
Without deceiving or having self-doubt,
Leadership requires strength from within
Only the call will bring it out.

LISTEN TO THE WINDS

Listen to the winds
And the stories they tell,
The size of the breezes
Begins to swell.
With love stories, secrets,
Whispers and lies,
Of tragedy, and hope
Someone is born and someone dies.
Form all around us
The lore is swept in the wind,
From cities and towns
Or a neighboring bend.
As the gusts go by
Sweeping far and near
They will whisk up your story
For others to hear.
If indeed by chance you happen to hear mine,
Yours will be along shortly
Somewhere in time.

LOVE

A declaration of expression
Of which there is no doubt,
Of people falling in
And lovers falling out.

Enchanting the world
Since the beginning of time,
In songs, and stories
Poetry and rhymes.

Even now it remains
Still a mystery,
Of how it alters the course
Of history.

In positions of power
Where changes were forbidden
Enticing men's hearts
And mad they were driven.

It has taken its toll
On all alike,
And buried the souls
Refusing to fight.

Make no mistake about it
You will definitely face,
And you'll know when love
Has left its trace.

LOVE STORY

In books and movies
And legends of old
Are the heartbreaks and happy endings
Of stories told.
Lovers left to their fate
And their journey's heart,
Either joined together
Or torn apart.
These are the realities
That we see, hear, and read,
Confirming our suspicions
For satisfying the need.
To love and be loved
As the saying goes,
Am I lucky in love?
No one knows.
No pain, no gain
No guts, no glory,
Do not live through them
Create your own love story

Vernon A. Nealy

MISSING YOU

Void of the moisture in the grass
When the day begins anew,
Dry to the touch, hard and brown
Because there is no dew.

Gone is the rainbow from the sky
After an evening shower,
It does not appear though the sky is clear
As I count each passing hour.

The gentleness of a breeze
On a warm summer's day,
I wait and I wait
But it comes not my way.

The dew and the rainbow,
Along with the breeze
The grass, the sky,
And even the trees

Together these things
Are only a clue
I miss them very much
But even more missing you.

ONE MORE DAY

You sit alone with private thoughts
Contemplating yesterday,
Remembering what your heart has felt
And what it was you wanted to say.

But instead your thoughts you hold inside
Not wanting to express,
Intense emotions deep within
This time allotted is not the best.

Tomorrow starts the day anew
You are granted another chance,
Take this time to think it through
And not just one quick glance.

But if your decision is to withhold
And your heart just cannot say,
Use this time to think again
Or take just one more day.

Vernon A. Nealy

OUR CIRCLE OF PRAYER

Our Father, we come together
Uniting hearts that care,
Bring you our petitions
Before your throne in prayer.

This day which you have granted
We know not what it holds,
But grace and mercy we ask of thee
As this dawn unfolds.

Prepare our hearts and minds with love
While maintaining a spiritual pace,
Our walk, service and conduct reflect
Our speech that is seasoned with grace.

Bless our families, friends and coworkers alike
And the children in our care,
Until we come together again
Uniting our circle in prayer.

REMEMBERING

As the dust settles
The memories will fade
Of all the old friendships
And acquaintances we've made.

But once in a while
You will catch a glimpse
Of a person you knew
Through the hole in the fence.

The fence represents duration
And how quickly it passes,
Memories made now
In time, become ashes.

Except for the ones
That we cherish in part,
Remembering them deeply
Within our hearts.

Vernon A. Nealy

SOUNDS OF SILENCE
THE SOUND OF GOD

The sounds of silence
Are clear as a bell,
The whispers of nature
Its beauty, its smell.
The colors and tapestries
Set an impressive stage,
A truly wondrous event
Which God has made.
See the heavens reflect
He is at the helm,
The past, present, and future
All eternity is His realm.
All for His glory
And testimony to show
He is still on the throne
And wants us to know
All this and more
To share in His delight,
Our creator's vision
And eternal light.

SUPPORT

I may not know what you're going through
But you have my undying support,
An arm to lean on, a shoulder to cry on
A friend and also consort.
You stand not alone
I'm ever present at your side,
To reverberate the laughter
Or shelter your cry.
To be strong when you are not
Helps to better pave the way,
It's a road to regain sure footing
And conquering the tasks of the day.
As for tomorrow, it's not promised
But if it comes I'll help you to sort
The problems and entanglements of that day
I'll be there for your support.

SWEET THINGS

It's the taste of succulent honey
With which your kisses are laced.
Warm and deeply satisfying
Sweet and wet to the taste.

It's the way you arrange and garnish
In preparing every meal,
The thoughtfulness behind it all
Provides the warmth I feel.

It's the way you take my hand
With reassurance and a gentle squeeze,
Lets me know you're right beside
Puts my heart at ease.

Yes, these things are sweet
And given with commitment thereof,
The sweetest of the sweetest things
Is giving and receiving your love.

THE HEART

Of all the treasures
We tend to hold,
What's valued more than
Diamonds or gold?

It cannot be spent
Or traded off,
Bartering is not the service
Will not cover the cost.

It is more precious
Than treasures combined
Increases in value
With the passage of time.

If you've chosen the heart
Then yes, you are right,
Guard with all honesty
Against toil or strife.

Understanding its purpose
And doing what's right
Because out of the heart
Flows the essence of life.

THE KISS

Sensual by nature
Desirable at heart,
The language of love
Where passions start.

It can ignite the senses
Into a roaring flame,
Or become a subtle response
If that is your aim.

Taste and feel
The warmth that's wet,
An expression of longing
You will not soon forget.

Let the heart send a message
That the mind can't miss,
The ambience of love
Begins with a kiss.

THE SOUNDS OF ANGELS

The sounds of angels
You will never hear,
Though they dance and frolic
They reside quite near.
Overseeing the lives
Of people neglected,
The poor, the humble,
They are being protected.
The rich and powerful
What necessity do they have?
To think there is no need
Would be terribly sad.
Regardless of the setting
There will always abide
The sounds of angels
Somewhere at your side.

WINTER'S KISS

She lies so boldly
Outside my door,
Clothed in white raiment
She beckons once more.

An emotionless embrace
With her frigid heat,
Signaling to me
She wants to meet.

Though beautiful to behold
Her smile so pure,
Inviting are her tapestries
She wants me to tour.

As I dress to complement
Her finest attire,
She calls me away
From the warmth of my fire.

To experience once more
The stillness of bliss,
She greets me at the door
With a cold winter's kiss.

UNMISTAKABLE

You stand out in a crowd
Without your name being mentioned,
An applauding entrance into the room
Your presence commands the attention.

Grace complements your beauty
As you promenade the center aisle,
Their approval draws gently
Your warm and tender smile.

An angel sent from heaven
For the entire world to see,
Majestic and unmistakable
Standing here with me.

YOU ARE THERE

With understanding and time to listen
A somber heart begins to sing,
Melodies of life, which it loves
Once held tight but now must cling.

But you are there I know not why
Nor do I question your right to be,
Perhaps this song my heart does sing
Has led your heart to me

Because you are there, it eases the pain
It's reflected in my eyes,
Your tender touch and gentle smile
Hold back the tears I want to cry.

It's to you that I am grateful
Embracing my soul anew,
Helps to restore this heart to sing
Its melody now sings for you.

SECRETS

(se′ krit) adj. 1. Concealed from general knowledge or view.

Hidden information, which can serve to aid or condemn people or circumstances. Knowledge based on fact. Intelligence-gathering for the sole purpose of concealment, or to be used at a precise time. The letters listed here are a pool of applied wisdom, for the avoidance of trouble, or answers to questions involving a personal state of affairs.

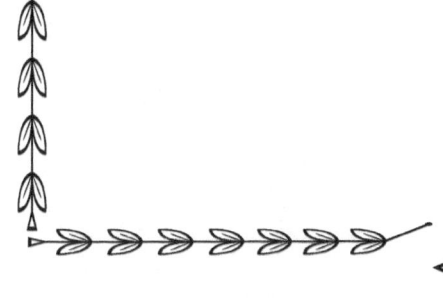

AGAINST ALL ODDS

Say it isn't so
Tell me it's not true,
All the cards within the deck
Are stacked solely against you.
Your back is against the wall
And you don't know what to do,
You've tried everything you can think of
But it's become a catch twenty-two.
Where do you go from here?
When standing in the road,
Do you turn left? Or do you go right?
Which way will lighten your load?
Take a breath, relax, and stand still
Regarding neither part,
Concentrate and listen
To the utterance of the heart.
Its decision will speak very softly
So listen to the choice
It's against all odds that you want to succeed
Now listen and follow that voice.
The long road back may be difficult
When wondering what to do next,
The journey of a thousand miles
Begins by taking the step.

AIRPORT

Wide-open spaces
Especially for you,
Neither a whisper nor a visit
Or anything passing through.
What will you do
To generate replication?
Make an effort to reach out?
Or send an invitation?
Realizing by now
The analogy made
Was just an example
Of a foundation laid.
The true intent
Never involved a plane,
Instead it refers
To an idle brain.
The danger lies
In the potential found,
Lacking motivation
Never leaving the ground.

ATTITUDE

A selected state of mind
And a word most often expressed,
Through sensibility of emotions
Or a position of unpleasantness.

But some of us fail to realize
The consequences of a negative stand,
The attitude displayed will be conveyed
As hostile, that people cannot stand.

Modify the mind as well as the heart
Becoming more tolerable without a doubt,
Chances are when a situation arises
It is more favorable of being worked out.

Success hinges on preparedness and timing
Ability and talent bring clout,
When competition is tough no need to get rough
Self-confidence will always win out.

BLIND

Listening to the people
I could visualize within my mind
Their chaos and the confusion
Seeking, hoping to find
Meaning in their lives
That requires some direction
Malice feeds immoral deeds
In need of total correction.
How can I without sight
Know this vision I have in mind,
Relying on my senses
It is they not I who are blind.

CHEATING

There are always some people
Willing to make this pledge,
Winning at all costs
The need to gain an edge.

Despite who's involved
While digging for dirt,
If you're in their way
You will surely get hurt.

It is all about the schemes
Filled with lust and greed,
A knife in your back
If you will not concede.

Be very careful about making this pledge
That your thoughts are never repeated
Blinded by the will to win
You may end up being cheated.

DEATH

Amongst the catacombs of life's deceased
Questions arise with shrouded answers,
Deep within the patriarch abides
The grim reaper and his dancers.
Come, inquire, seek, and discover
The response that suits your taste,
In so doing, you just might find
The replication that sealed your fate.
Death is permanent
You did the dance,
Pleasing is in vain
There is no second chance.
But you will never know
Until your last breath,
Your catacomb was labeled
For your place with death

DESPERATION

You are running out of options
As you wind around the bend,
Exhausting all possibilities
On a road that soon will end.

Now you are going to attempt
Something never tried before,
Wishing for much success
Or hoping to even the score.

Your brain is now held captive
Where logic does not apply
Your attitude has changed
It is reflected in your eyes.

Anxiety and grief have taken their toll
Banishing moral law,
A disregard for common sense
Which has broken the last straw.

All the signs are there
You have lost all concentration,
A meltdown now is eminent
Welcome to desperation.

DESTINY

From out of nowhere
Or so I thought,
A path was chosen
For me to walk.
My life extended
The normal realm,
Someone other than I
Was at the helm.
This journey before me
It stood in question,
Until I thought
Was all predestined.
The choices and circumstances
Were never in my hand,
Feeling guided and maneuvered
And part of a plan.
Until one day
I chose not to bend,
Realizing then my journey's end.
It has brought me closer
Fulfilling my sake,
And here I stand beholding my fate.
I knew not then
That it was she,
Hand in hand
With Destiny.

DO YOU HEAR OR DO YOU LISTEN?

Do you hear or do you listen?
Only one bears understanding,
After all that's said and done
Only one is ever demanding.
All that is truly needed
Is an investment of your time,
Allowing the words to process
And settle on your mind.
To hear is to respond
Acknowledging that you have heard,
In one ear and out the other
Comparable to a fleeting bird.
To listen is to interpret
Now hearing just to run,
But understanding the task at hand
Making sure the job gets done.
Do you hear or do you listen?
Have I made it perfectly clear?
The next time that you're spoken to
Try listening, not just to hear.

ESCAPE

For those of you
Who managed to flee,
From pursuit or disaster
Or harm to thee.
Understand this point
There are some who do not
Doomed by minutes even seconds
Disaster will claim their lot.
But a fortunate few
Will survive this time,
Only to be captured
At the end of the line.
To think it's not inevitable
Then there's a journey you must take
On a road that will lead to
Where there's no escape.

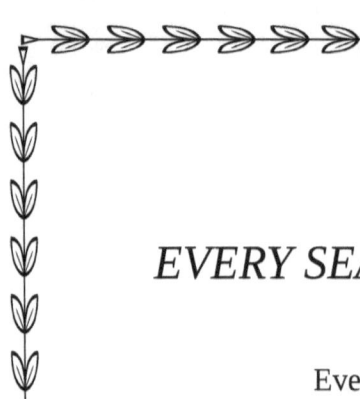

Vernon A. Nealy

EVERY SEASON HAS A FLAVOR

Every season has a flavor
That engages the human palate,
Either one or all a main course
That's offered with a tasty salad.
Our first dish begins with spring
That's warm and often pleasing,
Not much required in terms of dress
And very little seasoning.
Summer is our next entrée
It's hot with plenty of spice,
Beautiful beaches and clear blue waters
And the scenery is twice as nice.
Fall introduces the next delight
And for that we choose our seating,
With sports, birds, and pumpkin pie
It makes for real good eating.
Winter is the time for just desserts
When served it must be chilled,
Flowers and candy, gifts that are dandy
Even a heart would fit the bill.
So take your pick
Of a particular flavor,
Or indulge in all
A smorgasbord to savor.

FATAL

One of life's dreadful and altering words
We definitely do not want to hear,
It always targets the heart
With unrelenting fear.
It constantly numbs the mind
Preventing our thoughts to flow,
Grasping for any information
We do not wish to know.
Manufacturing a deranged state
Where you don't want to be,
Somewhat oblivious to life
As well as reality.
However, for now I will consider
To deal with the unwanted strife,
And to keep that word from invading
And interrupting my life.

FEAR

The empathy becomes immediate
Overwhelming and shockingly raw,
Whatever pierced your attention
Was something you felt or saw.

Paralyzed yet, you respond
As your emotions scrape the bone,
Clearly your brain understands
You're occupying a danger zone.

Your heart has been shocked with fright
In a grip of total embrace,
Your mind is frozen with panic
It displays quite well on your face.

Now, just like any circumstance
It may be possible for you to escape,
By quickly getting to safety
Or letting fear seal your fate.

Either way you'll know for sure
The impression it leaves never fades,
When you're in the perimeter of danger
You have a right to be afraid.

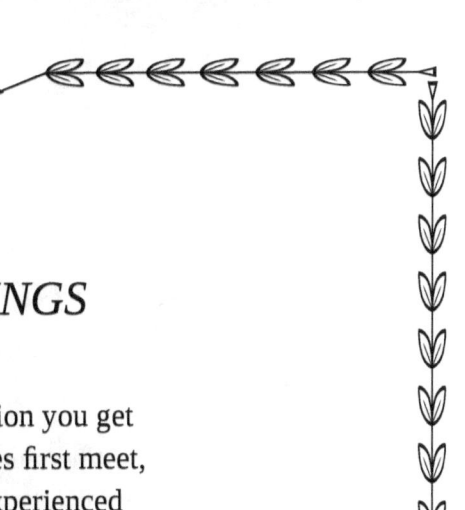

FEELINGS

It's the sensation you get
When your eyes first meet,
Vibrations experienced
From head to feet.

It touches the heart
And stimulates the mind,
That reaction you get
For the very first time.

To perceive an impression
And to have it appear,
At a distance of arm's length
So warm so near.

To know just what it is
With what you are dealing,
The heart comprehends and
Defines it as feelings.

FOR THOSE OF YOU

For those of you
Who clutch their tails
While passing through life
As though you have failed
By giving up now
You must realize,
You would be setting the stage
For your own demise.
Life is a gift
That is meant to be cherished
Not living without meaning
Just waiting to perish.
Grab hold of your hope
Gather and funnel,
Believe it or not
There's still light in your tunnel.
For those of you
Who are willing to give
Accepting this challenge
You will begin to live.
The choice now is yours
To stop or continue,
But for those of you
It is life on your menu.

FOREVER

Forever is a word
We casually throw around,
With matters of the heart
It means eternally bound.

An infinite design by choice
Once you've crossed the line,
Whatever you do you are committed
Till the end of time.

Be careful of what you say
Even more with one another,
And what position you find yourself
When speaking to others.

Keep in mind while expressing your thoughts
Forever you can't take back,
You must be cautious not to fall
In that forever trap.

FROM THE HEART

What the mind can conceive
The heart must believe
In order for the vision
To be achieved.

Motivation, inspiration
Are the springs from which they flow.
It all comes from the heart
If you really must know.

Your roots must be deep
And sincere from the start
With dedication and perseverance
You have a place to start.

Keeping in mind
That your dreams are real,
When they come from the heart
That seals the deal.

GOD

The most Holy Spirit,
The great I AM,
Creator of all Heavens
All life including man.
A majestic, righteous, and glorious judge
With love, mercy, and grace,
He stepped out of Heaven
To bear my sins
Redeeming and taking my place.
Glory to God and praise His name
In Him I often see,
In times of weakness and discontent
His strength will carry me.
Silly ideas and impossible dreams
These things I dare not chase.
Obedience and trust are what He commands
It is called walking by faith.
For those of you who do not quite know
And think this is just a façade,
I have just introduced to you, my friend
The omniscient and omnipotent God.

Vernon A. Nealy

HEART OF HEARTS

There is a place
I found as a youth,
It is deep within
And holds only truth.

It shines very bright
Alone and apart,
Only to be found
In the Heart of Hearts.

It divides the falsehoods
When your reasoning doesn't try,
And the mind is ready
To believe a lie.

Contrary to what's presented
Holding back or letting loose,
That light deep within
Contains only truth.

So before you answer
Look beyond your heart,
To the place deep within
Called the Heart of Hearts.

It is there that you'll find
Guilt has no place,
And the mask of respect
Shines bright upon your face.

I HEAR

Among the whispers and silent voices
People are found making choices
Rumors are spreading on the wings of fear
Trying to mask it although I hear.

Aside from the crowd with shifty eyes
Others point fingers as they pass by
What does it all mean? It is not quite clear
Trying to mask it even though I hear.

Amid the sounds, murmurs and coos
Avoiding at all cost the telling of truths
My sanctity now has been compromised
By indiscretions and telling of lies.

Never again to be so near
To someone I thought was a friend so dear
What does it all mean? It is not quite clear
Trying to mask it even though I hear.

IF WALLS COULD TALK

If walls could talk
The things they would say,
Of social or personal encounters
Of any particular day.

Secrets and lives exposed
True characters unmasked,
No rose-colored glasses
To hide your task.

People would learn
Of your true intent,
And hidden agendas
They would definitely prevent.

If walls could talk
Of schemes devised,
Where could you run to
Or even hide?

But, we know they don't
So you won't have to pant,
Talk they do not,
Aren't you glad they can't?

IN THE EYES THEREOF

If beauty is consequential
Then attraction is the start,
A natural association
Involving matters of the heart.

Emotions begin to surface
Overriding logical thought,
A disregard for protocol
Not applying what's been taught.

It's a level of profound ascension
In a realm where the eyes do feast,
Imagination and reality collide
Which will you seek?

To call it infatuation
Or see it as true love,
The answer lies within the heart
Or in the eyes thereof.

Vernon A. Nealy

IT HAD TO BE LOVE

There comes a time at our patience's end
When we are about to explode,
Logic is gone our anger is strong
And now we're about to unload.
It's at that time when the brain shuts down
And things become totally sober,
Emotions defused no verbal misuse
Our heart has taken over.
A safety valve that releases the pressure
And keeps our sanity intact,
Reminding us how control is important
In preventing a dangerous act.
As we take a look at what might have happened
And what were we thinking of,
It's at that point our heart intervened
Knowing it had to be love.

KEEPER OF SECRETS

As keeper of secrets
Of which I will not tell,
Silencing the whispers
Before they swell.

Muting all rumors
That circulate like fire,
Starving to death
The lies of desire.

As guardian of hearts
With lives at stake,
Protecting futures from ruin
So no secrets escape.

As keeper of secrets
Entrusted to my care,
Whether they're right or wrong
Or what's even fair.

I'm not to judge
And neither are you,
But, if you have a secret
I'll guard that too.

LADY OF THE LAKE

She welcomes my presence
With a silent applause,
Lady of the lake
Which nature has caused.
The smile she gives
So big and so bright,
Can only be seen
By the sun's shimmering light.
"Come, sit with me.
Take your place at my Nile,
Enjoy the tranquility
Stay for a while."
A most gracious host
As the wind strokes her surf,
One of the oldest daughters
Of precious Mother Earth.
As our conversation ends
I prepare to take my leave,
I rise from her banks
From spending time on my knees.
I thank her with a smile
For an ear she did lend,
A new friend I've made
I will surely come again.

THE LADY REVISITED (O.Y.L.)

Another year has come and gone
It is for her company I do yearn,
Longing to sit once again upon her banks
She graciously applauded my return.
So much to talk about
As we share our time,
In the absences between us
The months were kind.
Exchanging grand pleasantries
In our days of glory,
Laughing silently
At each other's stories.
She's become more than a friend
Protecting my secrets, careful not to uncover,
Occupying that special place
My heart, and fantasy lover.
Lady of the lake
Your beauty still abides,
Wherever life takes me
I'll never venture far from your side.

LEFT UNSAID

Discrepancies may often fuel
The flames of discontent,
If anger and attitude begin to sizzle
You have lost your common sense.

Your brain becomes overheated
By those thoughts inside your head,
Evolving into a poisonous venom
That your mouth is spewing instead.

Now it's too late to take it back
The damage has already been done,
Hearts become ice and feelings grow cold
It is you they choose to shun.

So take the time to think before
Let wisdom prevail instead,
To avoid unpleasant situations
Some things should be left UNsaid.

LONELY DREAMERS

Lonely dreamers have
A stage all their own,
The applause is for them
And for them alone,
A star of the show
Produced by one
Void of rivalry and upstaging
Having all the fun.
It can be very sad at times
But no one will know
You are the only person
Who attends the show.
Therefore, you smile
While holding back the tears,
Never having an audience
Throughout the years.
Nevertheless, you will never retire
At any age,
As long as you have
Your private stage.

LOST

It's a feeling which engulfs the senses
Quite foreign and overwhelming at times,
The ability to recognize and identify
Has been clouded and shut down your mind.

You cannot remember the things that you must
And what you do just doesn't pertain,
Without recollection, there is no retrospection
You are helpless alone in this frame.

Nevertheless, if you listen there might be a way
It's a secret that's quietly kept,
Stop! Turn around, observe your ground
Go back and retrace every step.

Your timing at this point is critical
For it depletes what memory you hold,
So proceed with caution this warning
It is the only way to regain control.

If by now, you still do not remember
Every road you possibly have crossed
My thought is, and I am not a whiz
You are definitely, definitely lost.

MATTERS OF THE HEART

Love and its relationships
Can be quite difficult at times,
An ongoing struggle for control
Can be yours and sometimes mine.

Instead, let us reach an accord
And affirm our love in part,
Take the time with understanding
Concerning matters of the heart.

Opposition will indeed arise
Like conflicts often do,
Keeping in mind our loving pledge
And courage will carry us through.

So I will say with sweet surrender
I am giving you my part,
Within our hands we hold the key
To matters of the heart.

ME

What I discovered in the mirror
That person looking back,
Just how little I really know
And just how much I lack.

Upon further observation
I felt I was being mocked,
Where lies are of no consequence
And secrets have no locks.

What lies behind the theatrics
That people seldom see?
It's what I just discovered
A revelation staring back at me.

MEMORIES

Thoughts of time long since gone
Warm the heart for a while,
Emotions are lifted, stress has drifted
Raising the corners of your smile.

Life, family, and friends remembered
Experiencing the good as well as the sad
Invites a tear that touches the heart
Embracing the warmth you have always had.

Memories are our resource in life
For which we generally find
Reflections of the stages of life
Reminiscing is often kind.

Hold on to those treasures
For they strengthen all hope,
Taking on the challenges
Allowing us to cope.

Memories are real and forever
Of this you can be sure,
There will often be an opportunity
For always making more.

NAMES

Reaching out to touch,
Identify, or claim,
You must be willing
To call it by name.
Names are by which
We relay our pitch,
Attaching to us the ownership.
Items of value
Sentimental or financial,
Indicate to others
It is very substantial.
A house, or property,
A roll of the dice,
Everything has a name
Even the love of your life.
Whether it is an autograph
Or monogram, even a recital,
You will recognize and appreciate
When you address it by title.
So, communicate your petition
Moreover, stake your claim
What belongs to you?
Call it by name.

OPULENCE & ROMANCE

A world we often dream about
Where very few of us live,
A fairy-tale fantasy for others
With wealth and power to give.

Opulence staggers the imagination
Where any need is obtained,
The urge to fulfill a single whim
To have it just call it by name.

Romance embraces the heart
With the grandeur of it all,
To love and be loved for the asking
To have at your beck and call.

It's a world I often wonder
Given the chance could I enfold,
Despite the beauty and splendor
There is a side that is gritty and cold.

But for now I'm content just where I am
To look and observe from a glance,
I'll continue to feed this fantasy
The world of opulence and romance.

POTENTIAL

Potential is a word
We often hear,
But for some of us reading
Its meaning is not clear.

To plainly understand
You must first confide
In your heart of hearts
Deep down inside.

What can I do?
How can I find the lift?
Discovering your potential
Is to discover your gift.

Grasping it tight
With all your soul
Using it well
To achieve your goal.

Motivate, enunciate
This gift is yours
Sharpen with discipline
And it will open doors.

Either that, or sit back
Maybe it is inconsequential,
But you'll never determine
Your true potential.

REMEMBER

Thoughts of times
Long since passed,
Memories of warmth
Forever last.

Golden dreams
Locked away,
Build with love
Day by day.

Secrets are kept
And locked with a key,
Their memories are hidden
Away from thee.

To unlock the future
Is an impossible task,
The key to remembrance
Lies in the past.

RHYTHMS OF LIFE

The rhythms of life
At first are not set,
Until our disciplines
Must first be met.

The harmony we seek
Of strong versus weak,
Determines the knowledge
That experience will teach.

When age and wisdom
Are then applied,
Seeking their level
Our rhythms will rise.

Dialoguing will help
As it leads the way,
If on your journey
You happen to stray

When you find your rhythms
And having no doubt,
It is locating the melody
You must think about.

SEDUCTION

It starts with a manifestation
We all somehow acquire,
Igniting our passion
And the object of desire.

Be it person, place, or thing
It will challenge every sense,
Feeding the mind and heart
Becoming progressively intense.

Whether you are hunter or prey
It is all the same,
Regardless of status
You are part of the game.

Where rules don't apply
And sometimes not fair,
Seduction is all around us
It permeates the air.

STIRRED NOT SHAKEN

Stirred not shaken
Refers to the way we look at life,
Our success and our victories
Along with the toil and strife.

Shaking can be violent
If you permit it, it will occur,
Leaving no room for peace
Which could be reached if easily stirred.

Nevertheless, people live their lives
In a way that they see fit,
Continuing to further press on
Or simply just to quit.

Now take for an example your life
Could be the martini that often occurs,
If you heed this fact and remember that
Not shaken but easily stirred.

STRONG MIND NOT, A WRONG MIND

To all young men
Who want to eagerly find
Their value in society
It is contained in these lines.
It transcends every culture
Boundary and walls,
Builds lasting respect
That unifies all.
It requires a will
That must break a mold
Of immoral attitudes
Of things taught or told.
Replaced by a mind
That desires to be strong,
A heart that rejects
Those things which are wrong.
Re-educating oneself
Will be the first thing to do,
Treating others as you
Would have them treat you.
This choice demands
Discipline and prayer,
To make this transition
You have to learn to care.
Humanity needs to know
For the future of posterity,
The changes you make
Will be in all sincerity.

SUCCESS

The formula for success
Is not difficult to find,
It requires patience and persistence
As well as much of your time.

Knowing what to choose
And the area of concern,
Let your gifts lead the way
Listen to them and learn.

For what comes easy to express
Very natural they all say,
They are your gifts revealing themselves
In a most obvious way.

Not necessarily monetary
Nor an accumulation of possessions,
It's the knowledge applied and learned
With the wisdom of life's lessons.

For God has granted you
An ability along with a test,
You have heard the prose, now reach and expose
Your gifts that lead to success.

SWEET DREAMS

The sweetest place I have found, it seems
Is locked away within my dreams,
Where imagination becomes so bold
Taking shape under my control.

I can fly through the clouds on a moment's notion,
Or swim with dolphins in the deepest ocean.
I can walk through a palace where kings have met,
Or alone on a balcony as your Juliet.

I can invite you in and set a mood,
Or enjoy the tranquility of my solitude.
But, to enter my dreams your heart must surrender,
While I create a fantasy that is soft and tender.

An assimilation of the minds is how it's done
Our physical consciousness will immerge as one
Time has no place when our two hearts meet,
Welcome to my world where the dreams are sweet.

THE AUGURY ROSE

There is a rose I've heard of
That's beautiful as well as rare,
It touches the hearts of lovers
Two people willing to share.

A lifetime together of nurturing
Helping each other to grow,
Becoming one unified spirit
That is when the rose will show.

What makes this rose so special
Is the attribute it does possess
Once found and held within its core
You are granted happiness.

But really, does such a rose exist?
Is it real or just a myth?
The answer lies somewhere in time
Are you willing to take the risk?

THE ROOT

The chief foundation of the soul
Can be taught and trained in character,
Whether it's in a positive or negative sense
Herein lies the factor,
To teach and train with counsel
In discipline and correction thereof,
Gentleness guided by wisdom
Will always provide the love.
To a character that grows progressively strong
It springs from a mighty root,
Through life's trials and treacherous storms
Always producing good fruit.
On the other hand,
With neglect and no supervision
And the rod is a forgotten measure,
Your hopes and dreams will sink
Disappear like sunken treasure.
Life's circumstances are magnified
When you're rubbing nose to nose,
Accountability will exact its toll
On you and even those.
Even hope is not lost
When you realize it's producing bad fruit,
The only solution left to seek
Is to pull up and kill the root.

Vernon A. Nealy

THE SOUND OF CHILDREN

There are very few sounds
That warm the heart,
Like listening to the sea
Or the singing of a lark.

There's also another
Which always transcends
Any boundaries or cultures
With the power to mend.

That is the sound of children
With laughter or at play,
Bringing joy to the heart
On any given day.

Sit by an open window
Or walk through the park,
Listen with intent
And your smile will start.

God's gift to the world
Provides a loving piece of art,
The sound of children
Really does warm the heart.

TIME

A measurable and constant duration
By which we think and plan,
The present as well as future
But is it all within our hands?

The best we can do with what we have now
Is to plan and use it well,
Whatever the task, successful or not
Only a period will tell.

Time holds the secrets
We would like to unfold,
Man's feeble attempts
At reaching that goal.

Twenty-four hours a day
Is all that we are given,
To journey forth on a steady course
In trying to earn a living.

Sleeping, eating, relaxing and work
Can we squeeze in anything else?
Whatever your decision on any condition
You have the time to decide for yourself.

TRY

You're the only reason
If failure starts to show,
You look to others for answers
But no one seems to know.

How much more effort
Are you really willing to try?
Don't reach that point of no return
And stop asking why.

But listen to that inner voice
Located deep within,
Give yourself another chance
Now try it once again.

Buried inside you have a light
That masquerades as doubt,
Use your talents and your skills
To bring it up and let it out.

Realizing now how blessed you are
And you're the reason why,
Refusing to be defeated
Now give it one more try.

UPSIDE DOWN

In this world,
Our journey is set,
We choose our path
That directs our steps.

But, there has been known
On distinct occasions,
It is upside down
We find our equation.

The best laid plans
May often fail,
When blown aside
By a windy gale.

Fear not at heart
However, try it again,
Reposition your anchors
And dig them in.

Hold on and pull tight
Not depending on luck,
Choose another path
That is right side up.

WHO AM I

Who am I?
On this road we call life,
A journey through time
Filled with chaos and strife.

Through bridges and tunnels
Gates and doors,
There are walls and ceilings
Windows and floors.

The choices are many
Which one should avail?
Afraid of success
Even worse, I could fail.

Let the choices remain
Until I discover,
What lies in my heart
Only time will uncover.

It's only then that I will know
Facing a limitless sky,
What type of person I have become
And discovering who I am.

WORDS

A vocal means of communication
Of how we sometimes feel,
An expression of thought that's verbally expressed
And what the heart reveals.

Words can soothe and restore emotions
As we occasionally may find,
Or stir the passions deep within
Adding stress that angers the mind.

Words can please and be used to heal
Building bridges and friendships that link,
Words can be harsh and often hurt
If we only take time to think.

Words in all languages get the point across
When cultures may sometimes fail,
It's words that are used in the state of affairs
Often lifting or removing a veil.

There is no magic, mystery, or shroud
Or a command of speech per se
But assessing circumstances for what they are
And choosing the right words to say.

YOU DON'T CARE

Your reputation precedes you
But you say that it's not fair,
Unjustly being labeled
As a person who doesn't care.

Somehow you fail to understand
And you say I have the nerve?
It's an established fact you've turned your back
On people you could have served.

That qualifies you as a careless person
Your character will always be questioned,
The accusations made and the foundation you've laid
Have no grounds for any objection.

Face the truth for what it is
I am only being fair,
When dealing with people you're quick to learn
That some of them just don't care.

LIES

(li´) n., Pl. A deliberate falsehood, image or impression.

Deliberate fabrication or distortion that can alter the course or outcome of people's lives and/or circumstances. It's inaccuracy guided or invented for the purpose of deception. This section deals with rumors, half-truths, dishonest images, and false impressions.

Vernon A. Nealy

ARE THERE REALLY MONSTERS?

Are there really monsters?
Children have asked and said,
They are hiding in my closet
Or just beneath my bed.

Awesome ghoulish creatures
Who await the cover of night,
Anticipating that moment
To give a child a fright.

Yes, there really are monsters
Not the ones in a fairy tale,
But those who society deemed a menace
And are locked away in jail.

Sexual predators and kidnappers alike
Nightmares filled with disgust,
No ghoulish fangs or pointy teeth
Just a devilish smile to win their trust

So, when asked do monsters really exist?
They need the truth from you,
The undesirables in our society
Yes, they really do.

BETRAYAL

When loyalty becomes seditious
It brings a horrid change,
Rising to an anxiety level
Somewhere between shock and pain.

Your body now becomes livid
While your mind is in total denial,
To maintain composure and control
It's going to take awhile.

Don't relinquish reasoning
It doesn't mean they have won,
All it means is that your trust was violated
And it happened—what's done is done.

Now guard your heart
Build a wall if you must,
But check again
Your circle of trust.

For the seeds of deception
Are blown in the wind,
If you're not attentive
It may happen again.

CONTROL

A dangerous and curious objective
That caters to the flesh,
Giving into the desire of
Changing your worst to its best.

Your intentions may be honorable
When you take the reins at first,
It intoxicates the senses
While the power feeds the thirst.

You're now engaged in assimilation
Gorging into the fold,
The harder you struggle to ease the alliance
Influence is taking control.

The disaster you fear is imminent
And the part that's really sad
It was the power and prestige you were really after
But control you never had.

FLIRTING

Harmless or playful intentions
But you're really out to win,
If you think flirting is cute
Then think and think again.

You are courting an unhealthy intent
That carries a heavy load,
It's like lighting a match to a fuse
That will eventually explode.

Of course it's not your intention
Misleading with your cooing,
To say you have it under control?
You don't know what you're doing.

No one wants to be labeled
A knucklehead or a jerk,
But trust me, people, on this
Someone will definately get hurt.

For the men and women who read this
And your wandering eyes still roam,
You'll be much better off to listen
And leave the flirting alone.

GARDEN OF LIES

It begins with the planting
Of a single seed,
A thought of deception
Or ominous greed.
Cultivating all of society's desires
Endless falsehoods and obsessions,
Evades the truth and moral standards
Turning away from valuable lessons.
The seedlings of lies
Begin to spread,
Obvious fabrications
Inside their heads.
A multitude's preoccupation
Introduced by aristocracy,
Watered by deceit
That nurtures hypocrisy.
No matter how hard
To escape we try,
Our society will cultivate
Its garden of lies.

MORE THAN YOU CAN CHEW

The smorgasbord of life
May look temptingly pleasing,
But a carefree indulgence
Is dangerously misleading.
So much to choose from
And so much to do
You'll take and take and take some more
Of whatever's in front of you.
Keeping in mind the risk you run
Of choking on a skewer,
For which there is no remedy
Or Heimlich maneuver.
A fatal feast for the glutton
Who fails to realize,
Now you've gone and done it
You have sealed your own demise.
Heed these words of caution
Think in all that you do,
Be careful not to bite off
More than you can chew.

Vernon A. Nealy

OPENING YOUR MOUTH

When it comes to the truth
There can be no doubt,
Think before you speak
When opening your mouth.

You will be judged accordingly
Your integrity is on a wire,
Say the wrong thing
You will be labeled a liar.

Many a reputation
Has been cast to the side,
He who has crossed that line
Their character has died.

So when it comes to the truth
There can be no doubt
Think before you speak
When opening your mouth.

PLAYING BY THE RULES

Life is a game
Is the way some people feel,
They do not take it seriously
Enough to be real.

They step out of bounds
And act like a fool,
They swear they're all that
While ignoring the rules.

Anything you say
They do not want to hear,
And if you step up to challenge them
They want to rule you by fear.

But their day will come
When they're taken to school,
Learning the hard way
To play by the rules.

Vernon A. Nealy

POWER, PRIVILEGE, AND JUSTICE

With power and privilege
To all take heed,
They embrace responsibility
Of a virtuous need.

To the rich and powerful
Powerless and poor,
Producing a mind-altering status
With an erroneous core.

They can become deceivingly gratifying
Quite a palatable décor,
Not knowing when to stop
And always wanting more.

It is a lie you will regret
Having no escape,
With power and privilege
Justice will assimilate.

PREMEDITATED

The evidence is in
It was not as you stated,
The indications show
It was premeditated.
The lies you've told
Manipulating the truth,
Unbeknown to you,
You have fashioned your noose.
It was intentional, deliberate,
Prearranged and then mended,
Hiding your motives
To which your heart intended.
Thinking things through
For revenge or condition
Places you in
A precarious position.
So, abandon all notions
Of the evil you have contemplated,
For when the truth is revealed
It will not be premeditated.

PRETTY WOMAN?

You have a strut to your walk
That's graceful as a gazelle,
Shown with pride and dignity
Everyone can tell.
Your hair is soft as silk,
As it dances in the breeze
A frame that's voluptuous
All 360 degrees.
Eyes that captivate
A smile so enchanting,
An air of mystery
Makes it all the more inviting.
But I looked even deeper
Than your exterior would reveal,
Only through conversation
The layers began to peel.
You're empty and self-righteous
Conceited and pretentious,
Void of qualities of warmth
Just cold and venomous.
To others you may be
The pretty woman they see
Pretty isn't the word I'd use
You are very ugly to me.

PROPHECY

Foretold in the past
By our history's seat,
The lessons not learned
We're doomed to repeat.
Predictions that await
Mankind's fate are not new,
Without intervention
It will all come true.
Prejudice and bigotry
The malice we accept
All filters down
To a tone of disrespect.
Humanity's last call
Before the fat lady's dance,
If we fail to respond
There will be no olive branch.
You make the decision
It starts with you
Is this prophecy false
Or will it all come true?

REGRET

Life offers no invitations
Or a special place in line,
The first to come is the first to be served
Is what you will often find.
Do not make an excuse to sleep
Or daydream excessively much,
You will find yourself recumbent
Or buried in a rut.
Decisions I know are many
The right ones are only few,
Examine all conclusions
And choose the one for you.
Keep in mind the value
Of the end result you set,
If you let it go or slip away
You will snivel with regret

REQUIEM FOR LOVE

The final tear at last was shed
So now this story can be told,
Of a love reminiscent but savored not
And how it had grown progressively cold.
It began with the warmth
Both hearts entrusting,
Faithful and secure
Supporting and loving.
Loyalty and trust
Were the ties that bind,
Protecting and nurturing
Each other through time.
Until it was discovered
Where temptation nested,
Love you don't trust
Until it's been fully tested.
Taken for granted
Our roles were not clear,
Our loyalty challenged
And trust disappeared.
In a moment of fragility
A new chapter was written,
A time-honored tradition
As our hands became smitten.
Do not look for a resolution
Or an answer being rescinded,
The damage sustained in paradise
Will not at this time be mended.
And so ends this chronicle
Its choices and lamenting thereof
Avoid everything that temptation may bring
Or experience the requiem for love.

RIGHT OR WRONG

When approaching the issues
You must understand,
The morals and ethics
Before taking a stand.
It is not cut and dried
As one might believe,
Or going back and forth
To gain a reprieve.
Nor rationalizing the problem
To justify a means
Made to look unimportant
Or so it seems.
What's right or what's wrong
Doesn't come from the mind,
It is found in the heart
Each and every time.
So, understand each issue
And search deep in your soul,
Then what's right or what's wrong
Will begin to unfold.

SINS

You have fashioned a world
With treachery and deceit,
On the unsuspecting victims
You've come to meet.
Though heartless and cruel
The tides now have turned,
You are the victim
Now you must learn.
It's not a trial or retribution
Or vengeance you must face,
But the sins of one relentless heart
That chose malice in its place
Stand ready to receive in full
The total measure of your deeds,
The cruelty you have so readily displayed
Shall bring you to your knees.
The verdict will be hard to swallow
It will serve for the rest of your time,
Beginning with loyalty, honesty, and justice
You will love all mankind.

SLAVE

I bear no chains
Shackles or ropes,
I do not ravage my body
With drugs or dope.
Yet, in my desires
I have a constant need
This uncontrollable urge
On which to feed.
The impulse I feel
My fibers corrode
Rest is beyond reach
In my mental abode.
Tortured and beaten
Nevertheless, no one sees
A slave to my desires
I live on my knees.
Entertaining the thoughts
Not big or bold,
But held long enough
To enslave my soul.
The key I think
To winning this bout
Before thoughts become engaging
Quickly get them out.

SOLVING THE WORLD'S PROBLEMS

It begins with all of the issues
One problem at a time
Before I begin to help the world
I will start by dealing with mine.
I know their burdens are heavy
Their hearts are filled with pain,
To assist this cause for people
Lift them up
And out of their shame.
Return the dignity that they once knew
Lifting their heads with pride,
By guaranteeing them the right to choose
They would refuse any freedom rides.
Respect of differences and understanding
Shows what diversity can bring,
A foundation that's strong and unified
And a culture that's ready to sing.
So now, I go back to all of the issues
One problem at a time,
Before I begin to help the world
I'll start by dealing with mine.

Vernon A. Nealy

STICKS AND STONES

There is a child's rhyme
That is easy to recite,
Created as a deterrent
So boys and girls won't fight.
That was then, this is now
The same does not hold true,
Sticks and stones will break your bones
But names can definitely hurt you.
Examine the psychology
Of a child with low esteem,
When children use names to inflict such pain
They are just downright mean.
The scars they will bear
From the vicious verbal attacks,
As adults—in later years
It will all come rushing back.
Antisocial misfits
With a bloody axe to grind,
"You called me names, it's your bones I now claim!"
You have been warned that these are the signs.
Names can hurt, worse than a fist
After the pain has gone,
With criticism and constant maligning
You hinder them from growing strong.
Knowing that sticks and stones will hurt
It is your thinking you must manage
You must think twice, using words that slice
Or you will end up perpetuating the damage.

TEACHING A CHILD'S HEART

A lot has been said
Even less has been felt,
The innocence we're given
Exposed on a shelf.
A gift from the Master
Our Creator up above,
To be molded with caring,
Forgiveness and love.
It unconditionally accepts
Duplicity or truth,
You'll reap what you've planted
From the heart of that youth.
If you want to be loved
And respected with care
In your time of need
Will that child's heart be there?
Understanding this now
With love and tears,
A child's heart will be kind
In your golden years.

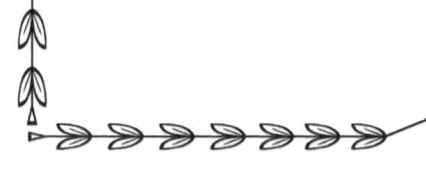

TEARS OF A CLOWN

You ride the winds of your folly
Now experience the lull of a breeze,
It is sadness calling attention
That knocks you to your knees.
It is always good while indulging
Playing roulette with foolish fears,
The gravity of your stupidity unloads
Now your eyes are filling with tears.
The wisdom absurd, advice unsound,
Instruction you chose to ignore.
The price you are paying, "I am sorry," you are saying
Lady pardon has locked her door.
Maybe now you will listen
To this doctrine which is sound,
Avoiding foolish folly
Evading the tears of a clown.

TEMPTATION

Its lure is very seductive
It is through eyes that you are caught,
A longing glance is all it takes
Your soul can now be bought.
Its charms ignite your fancy
Musing begins to unfold,
As passions swell within your chest
Temptation takes control.
Perception now becomes distorted
While tempting thoughts do come,
Descending from the mind to the heart
You know this deal is done.
For those of you who struggle
Hope is not necessarily lost,
Those seeking escape must keep in mind
The consequences that come with a cost.
A longing glance, forget it
Negative thoughts don't curtsy
This is the point where you must be strong
Or it will have you at its mercy.

THE ANNUNCIATION

As with most of us we wait to hear
Or see just what's in store,
My ship is coming or so we say
Until then my life is a bore.
But what we fail to comprehend
Is the question we often ask,
What if my ship does not arrive?
Can I still complete my task?
What is it that we are looking for?
Riches? Or undiscovered wealth?
Will lady luck smile on me?
Or will she smile on someone else?
Now stop—ponder for a moment
Are you waiting for your ship to come in?
Chances are it will never arrive
Because it is docked in the spirit within.
The annunciation was just announced
You have had it all the time,
You are the captain of your ship
And it's your destiny you have to find.
So pull up anchor and let us set sail
Straight to the forward bow
Your ship is here ready to cast off
And I think that time is now.

THE BRUSH

Its meaning may seem obscure
In the use of the term,
To understand this prose
Read and you shall learn.
It is a feeling you get
That is morbid and cold,
When the reaper stands close
To your mortal soul.
A grim situation
With no salutation,
Coming to claim his prize
And no explanation.
Caught off guard
In the middle of life?
From birth to present
It comes with a price.
The shock becomes hypnotic
No time to ask why me,
As the reaper gets ever so close
Only moments or seconds to flee.
The brain must fight paralysis
While the mind hatches a plan,
Fear becomes an overwhelming opponent
You defeat them any way you can.
All is a matter of moments
To understand the meaning of brush,
It happens so fast like a tornado's blast
You have escaped the reaper's rush.
By now your heart is pounding
You have managed to breathe your next breath,
Let's just say you were lucky this time
But you had a brush with death.

THE CHALICE

To drink from the cup
Where the spirits are high,
Quenching one's thirst
Which never runs dry

An elixir of love
That tastes—bittersweet,
Like the finest Chablis
Or the spoilage of meat.

The nectar is flavorful
And also tantalizing,
Its effects on mind
Hypnotic and mesmerizing.

To acquire a taste
Which suits your palate,
The decision you make
May become your habit.

But understand this
It cuts like a knife,
The chalice you choose
Will become yours for life.

THE FINAL SIEGE

As earlier battles were fought and won
She remained victorious and second to none.
On matters dealing with the heart,
Her final siege was yet to start.
A mistress of seduction she can be,
Stealing the mind and heart of me.
Yet, it is my advances she stops to seek
Halting my words before I speak.
Lest I forget, I shut my eyes
Focusing solely on my prize.
The thrill of the hunt as I centered my aim
Unbeknownst to me she invented the game
The odds now were no longer in my favor,
The sweetness of victory she began to savor.
With just one glance into her eyes,
My position now was compromised.
I realized then before I had begun
The final siege she had already won.

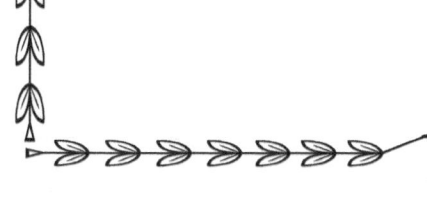

Vernon A. Nealy

THE GIFT

Time holds the answers
To all that we seek,
But generation upon generations
Have failed to keep
The wisdom that was learned
Of its people and their cultures,
While some became predators
And others became vultures.
This vicious cycle turns to blood
The innocent are slain
Who hears their cries?
Who feels their pain?
Now the answers you seek
Are not within these lines,
But back through the ages
Somewhere in time.
Or perhaps in history
You may yet discover
The wisdom that was learned
Is the gift still covered.

THE HUNGER

Chances are you will experience
A passion you cannot hide,
A longing for an approach to engage
Logged so deep inside.
Driven by the want
You will never concede,
Until you find a way
To fulfill that need.
A thirst, a craving, a desire so strong
A human attribute
That accompanies a song.
From within your core
You can feel the ache,
Must satisfy this appetite
For as long as it takes.
This urge is life
As the aspiration grows stronger
I must and I will
Fulfill this hunger.

THE JOURNEY

The journey for us
Begins at birth,
Traveling through
Our universe.
Our conscious mind
Void of thought,
Of our existence
From which we were brought.
Until such time
We escape the real,
Of our birth mother's womb
We are put at the helm.
As life is granted
We grow to find,
The reason for our journey
Somewhere in time.
Securing bits and pieces
We search for the rest,
While venturing on another journey
Which begins in death.

THE LIAR

Your heart is perverse
Your mind is corrupt,
The lives you have touched
Are all screwed up.
Now you open your mouth
Your speech is not sound,
It is void of the truth
Only fabrication is found.
You have become quite offensive
While trying to persuade,
Bringing both genders
Into a quarrelsome cascade.
I know who you are
And I am beginning to tire,
Your exploits have dubbed you
The habitual liar.

THE MASQUE

I wear many hats
For the roles that I play,
But you'll never know
When I come your way.

I am very pretentious
In gaining your trust,
A professional at work
I do what I must.

I can be a lover,
A brother, sister or mother,
When the situation calls for it
I can become any other.

But my true character
You will never see
Protected by guile
And the masque that hides me.

THE MASQUES OF HUMANITY

9/11/01, a day unlike any other
The faces of mankind were revealed,
Although we think and often ask why
The answers are painfully real.
Nineteen set a course
In which thousands would die,
With malice and animosity
They came from the sky.
The shock of it all
The lives that were lost,
America had paid dearly
What an awful cost.
The strongest nation on earth
Yet, accessible in every way,
That event has changed our lives forever
In how we live each day.
Vigilant, we must all become
In helping America mend,
Unmasking the faces of humanity
To find either foe or friend.
The nine-eleven memories will linger
So our nation must continue on,
Prayer, faith, God's good grace
Will keep America strong.

Vernon A. Nealy

THE PROVERBIAL LINE

The proverbial line
Does it really exist?
Real or imagined
Are you willing to risk?
Stepping across
To endanger your fate,
Protecting your pride
You may not escape.
Challenging the odds
Of what's left to prove,
Nothing to gain
But everything to lose.
The proverbial line
Requires much thought,
Remembering life's lessons
And the things you were taught.
Mistakes you avoid
And your pride you must swallow,
Ignoring sound wisdom
Only a fool would follow.
Honestly, is it really worth it?
Or just a waste of time,
To lose and lose again
That's the proverbial line.

THE VOID

Graphic in nature
And clear as a bell,
The grandeur of it all
Yet, people cannot tell.
It provides not a thing
Neither substance nor space,
And for most of us all
It is right in our face.
It stagnates the mind
That causes you to stare
Looking for something
That is not even there.
It's those little elapses of time
We zone into and stall,
Some people refer to it as a daydream
When asked, oh, it was nothing at all.

THIRTEEN

Of all the numbers to be savored
We all have one, a special favorite.
But there is another, under no condition
Should you allow its superstition.
Surrounded by uncertainty, a fearful cup,
Some believe very strongly produces bad luck.
But if you allow your mind to conceive,
Dwelling on the negative you will believe.
Bringing into reality your greatest fear
How one produces it is still unclear.
But this remember, keep your faith intact
If not, superstition will hold you back.

TRUTH

An ingredient for life
That is contrary to a lie,
It is a basis for integrity
And the reason why.
It will stand on its own
If covered will emerge,
It springs from the heart
Rather than staying submerged.
Its growth will increase
As it nourishes the mind,
With diligence, practice,
And the passage of time.
Endure this one principle
With no hesitation,
And build your life carefully
With a strong foundation.

UNCONVENTIONAL

Words that rhyme
Verses with rhythm
Seek to serve a purpose
In expressing our thoughts.
In matters of the heart
Emotions become intense,
In the positive or negative sense.
Energy that feeds me leads me to accomplish
My task. A task that is successful without a mask.
Is it unconventional, you ask?
Nonconformity, archaic, even unorthodox
Some might call it a paradox.
A need to vent, verses well spent
Understanding enlightened, now you know what I meant.
Life, accepting whatever comes,
Unable to hold on
It bears no thumbs.
Drop out, pop out, the choices will not dictate
Your journey, your walk, your favor
Does not rehabilitate.

URBAN LEGENDS

Urban legends,
Truth or fabrication?
A bite of reality
Or someone's imagination?
Stories that are told
With a mixture of truth
Gripping the mind
Not letting it loose.
Fear, caution,
It follows a design,
Verity, actuality,
Or more myth inclined.
You decide after hearing the plot
Judge for yourself
Whether it is real or not.
I'm just a voice
Taking a risk,
But urban legends do exist.

VAMPIRES

Nocturnal creatures on the hunt
In search of life and its appeal,
Gothic tales of love and horror
Exist today, this curse is real.
Their adoption of appearances
Will always play
An important part
In capturing their prey.
Sincere and honest
They claim to be.
With an ulterior motive
That you cannot see.
Murderers, thieves, and unscrupulous cons
Baiting their hooks with truth and lies,
Whether the sun is up or the moon is out
Vampires upon vampires will continually rise.

WINTER THOUGHTS

Winter thoughts how cold sometimes
Lodged so deep within my mind,
No one hears my private speeches
Alone I walk on frozen beaches.

Longing to feel the warmth of the sun
Instead in the frigid shadows I run,
In self-imposed exile I spend my time
Confronting secrets I do not want to find.

Still they are here among the whispers
Secluded thoughts and her sisters,
Yet, they tug, pull and so hard I fought
To remain within my winter thoughts.